Obstacles *to* Deliverance

Rev. Christopher S. Peterkin

Order this book online at www.trafford.com
or email orders@trafford.com

Most Trafford titles are also available at major online book retailers.

All scripture quotations and references are taken from the King James Version (KJV) published by Thomas Nelson Publishers

Printed in the United States of America.

ISBN: 978-1-4269-9390-9 (sc)
ISBN: 978-1-4269-9546-0 (e)

Library of Congress Control Number: 2011916820

Trafford rev. 10/05/2011

www.trafford.com

North America & international
toll-free: 1 888 232 4444 (USA & Canada)
phone: 250 383 6864 • fax: 812 355 4082

Contents

Acknowledgements

It is my obligation to acknowledge the God, most supreme over all the earth who has given me, not only the reason to live, but to live happily in His presence.

I have seen His presence, and I have experienced His favor throughout the writing of this book's pages. I was never lacking His grace and wisdom; eg, the gift of His Spirit was always close to behold, and bask in.

In Him, I always found comfort.

There are the words of one famous songwriter, who is believed to be now deceased, summarized this point in his words;

> What a friend we have in Jesus, all our sins and grief to bear.
> What a privilege to carry, everything to God in Prayer.
> Oh, what peace we often forfeit, oh what needless pain we bear.
> All because we do not carry everything to God in Prayer.

I can do nothing less than to bow down before Him in full reverence, and worship, for He has been my constant friend and support.

I have come to realize that writing a book consumes a lot of time, energy, focus and dedication from the author. That being the case, it is very important for me to acknowledge my wife for her patience and understanding.

As a result, I refuse to take her gift for granted. A monetary figure cannot be put to the value of her patience, her love and understanding.

Honey, thank you so much. You have contributed much in seeing this project through.

To the honorable, Dr. Alister R. Penny, I say thank you for the great work, and patience you've contributed into the accomplishment of this book.

Thank you very much for accepting my call to you, which might have been a challenge. To my niece Marcia, I say thank you very much for your wonderful skill and art work.

Introduction

The world's most famous and successful evangelist (Jesus Christ), once declared;

"Verily (truly) I say unto you; if you have faith and not doubt, you shall not only do this which is done to the fig tree, but also, if you shall say unto this mountain (your mountain, my mountain) be thou removed, and be thou cast into the sea, it shall be done.

And all things whatsoever you shall ask in prayer, believing, you shall receive." This you will find in the New Testament gospel book of Matthew 21:21-22.

Those are very strong words, not only strong, but true. They are real, because they are being experienced in the lives of many who exercise the quality of faith that is required.

If you use undoubting faith, (not second guess God) in addressing your situation, or condition, it shall be taken care of.

Remember though, one must be in good standing with Him, to whom he/she is praying.

Sin in a person's life, will always be a mountain standing against their faith, resulting in unanswered prayer. The healing which they desire, and the request they are making will not be answered.

I need to justify that statement to some of you, so look with me at a passage of scripture.

In Matthew 9:1-7; Verse two says; they brought to Jesus a man who was sick of palsy. In other words he was crippled, and could not have carried about himself. Wherever he went, he was dependant on others.

What did the sick man, and those who brought him to Jesus sought for? Healing, and deliverance from his (visible, and physical) condition, and what did Jesus gave him/them?

Jesus said; "Son, be of good cheer (not afraid, it is okay now); your sins are forgiven you."

This man's sins were the obstacle to him being healed of his condition.

That which Jesus did was queried by those around Him who witnessed the confrontation, and ultimate change in the sick man.

They saw Jesus as a blasphemer, who deceives the people, and cannot do what He says, because He does not possess (possess as they claim) the power nor the authority to do so, but God.

However, Jesus refuted their querying in verses five and six.

Jesus had power which they knew not of. Jesus has power, not only to heal the sick, but also to forgive sins.

This was proven before their eyes.

Jesus said to the sick of the palsy; "Arise, take up thy bed and go unto thy house."

In response, the no longer sick man, arose and went to his house.

It is appalling that some people are possessed with the idiocy to publicly discredit, and refute the authority of Jesus Christ.

Foolishness is not bound up in the heart of children only, but in adults too. Nevertheless, the word of the LORD, and His authority, that shall stand. Proverbs 22:15 & Matthew 16:17

Chapter One

The Obstacle, Sin

The Zondervan Pictorial Encyclopedia of the Bible, Copyright © 1975, define Sin as; guilt, and error, a failure, iniquity, trespass, transgression, fall.

The failure or refusal of human beings to live the life intended for them by GOD their creator.

The Eerdman's Bible Dictionary, first edition, definition of Sin is expressed as; an action, state which can be as missing the mark, fall, a transgression, to transgress, a revolt, perversion, to err, lawlessness, unrighteousness.

The American Heritage Dictionary, second collage edition, described Sin as; a transgression of a religious or moral law.

A condition of estrangement from God as a result of breaking God's law.

Sin is; an offense, violation, fault or error.

To every human being living upon the earth, and above the earth, even if they may be, beneath the earth, have faced and will conclude; Sin is perhaps older than anything else you've known.

It has been affecting humanity for more than even the many tons of food consumed by the body throughout one's lifetime.

Sin; as an action, many people experience pleasure, however, when finished is followed by guilt and emptiness. As a condition, many experience unhappiness. Ultimately, the end consequence for Sin is eternal separation of man from his creator.

The bible declares; "For the wages of sin is death, but the gift of God (Jesus Christ) is eternal life through Jesus Christ our Lord." Romans 6:23. Sin is an obstacle or barrier which hinders man, male or female from returning to God his creator in escape of the misery and unhappiness he experiences. Sin denies the body excellent health, and eventually starves it of life.

It interests me at this time to take a look at the gospel of Matthew 9:1-8. That passage speaks of Jesus, the gift of God, forgiving, and not only forgiving, but healing a young man who was sick of the Palsy. Palsy is a condition of the body in a paralyzed state. In the medical profession today, it will be said that he has paralysis, meaning, the individual lack the power, in some cases to feel or control movement in parts of the body. This should help one to better understand why this man was brought to Jesus as stated in the text. He was not supported with the use of crouches, but brought lying on a bed. This man obviously agreed to be brought to Jesus, and there are two reasons supporting that opinion. One, he knew that he had a need. Two, others believed that he had a need, and they all believed that Jesus, the gift of God was able to meet and satisfy that need.

This paralyzed man was seen as having two deficiencies. One physical, and the other spiritual. His physical condition was the result of his spiritual condition going bad.

Jesus, upon seeing the faith of those people, which is believed to be four of them, said to the paralyzed man; "Son, be of good comfort, your sins are forgiven you." Unlike Job, that great patriarch who was righteous and upright before God, was plagued with a severe sickness. Job 2:7. Job knew that he did nothing wrong which should result in the condition he was in. But this man under review seemed to have had no knowledge of the cause of his palsy. His approach too, was different to that of Job's approach.

Like many today, even as you read through these pages, there are those plagued with a sickness, and desire to be healed of it. The most likely decision made in such circumstances is, visit the doctor.

After visiting doctor after doctor, and consuming and applying the several prescribed medications, the condition remains, or grow worse.

Time seemed to have been quickly on the count down for this crippled man. Jesus, we know from the scripture was just visiting the area, not knowing when he was going to return after leaving.

Desperate situations require desperate measures, and so it was. Yet there are those who, in desperate situations do not posses the energy to make a desperate act. John 5:5-14

As this man, being a paralytic came to Jesus to be delivered from his physical condition, experienced, not only physical healing, but the sin which was the cause of his physical deficiency, was forgiven. He came to Jesus being carried on a bed, and left Jesus' presence carrying his bed. He was forgiven of his obstacle to deliverance.

If your condition is similar, and can relate to this man, then you too can have similar experience of healing.

James the disciple of Jesus Christ, in his writing of his epistle states in chapter 1:13-15; "Let no man say when he is tempted, I am tempted of God, (temptation and being tempted are always negative and emotional feelings and expressions. Being tempted, one is influenced to do wrong. Violating a right principle is what temptation works against) for God cannot be tempted with evil, neither tempts he any man. But every man is tempted when he is drawn away of his own lusts and enticed. Then when lust is conceived, it brings forth sin, and sin, when it is finished brings forth death."

James is saying that Sin, when manifested did not abruptly take place. There was a period through which the individual was influenced to commit the act. The Sin first acted or manifested itself on the person's emotional being.

In the beatitudes recorded in Matthew 5:28, Jesus said; "Whosoever looks on a woman to lust after her, has committed adultery with her already in his heart."

It can be shocking for many to know what goes on in a person's heart, very gruesome in nature.

The question is often asked; why are there so many more women in, and attending church than men? And why are men more prone to turn away from the gospel of Christ, and the gift of God when presented to him? The sin of the heart is cancerous, and can only be treated by and through Jesus Christ. The sin of man's heart is the biggest obstacle to him being a true representation of his creator, and not fulfilling his roles as a good father, husband, and leader.

Chapter Two

The Right Environment

I was sitting in a forum, where the subject of discussion was a diseased woman. At one point in the discussion, a statement was made, which I do not remember; however, it was like my mind being empty, was suddenly filled before realizing the situation, and enlightenment.

The moment was an over whelming one.

I then saw myself in relation to the sacrifice which Jesus Christ made for me and others, and the many obstacles which we allow to deny us the truth.

Isa. 53:4-7 declares; "Surely he hath borne our griefs, and carried our sorrows, yet we did esteem him stricken, smitten of God, and afflicted. But he was wounded for our transgressions, he was bruised for our iniquities, the chastisement of our peace was upon him, and with his stripes we are healed. All we like sheep have gone astray, we have turned every one to his own way, and the Lord hath laid on him the iniquity of us all. He was oppressed, and he was afflicted, yet he opened not his mouth. He is brought as a lamb to the slaughter, and as a sheep before her shearers is dumb, so he openeth not his mouth."

The gospel according to Mark, gives the account of a woman's sickness, and her moment of healing. This record you will find in chapter 5:25-34.

"And a certain woman, which had an issue of blood, twelve years.

And had suffered many things of many physicians, and had spent all that she had, and was nothing bettered, but rather grew worse.

When she had heard of Jesus, came in the press behind, and touched His garment.

For she said, if I may touch but His clothes, I shall be whole.

And straightway the fountain of her blood was healed of that plague.

And Jesus, immediately knowing in himself that virtue had gone out of Him, turned Himself about in the press, and said (by asking); Who touched my clothes?

And His disciples said unto Him; Thou seest the multitude thronging thee, and sayest thou, who touched me?

And He looked round about to see her that had done this thing.

But the woman fearing and trembling, knowing what was done in her, came and fell down before Him, and told Him all the truth.

And He said unto her, daughter, thy faith hath made thee whole; go in peace, and be whole of thy plague."

At the time of this event, there were various experiences, not only by the woman who was, most directly affected, but by those who witnessed the event.

The disciples of Jesus were among such a people.

The Pharisees were also numbered among them, and of course the skeptics.

I love the wisdom of the bible and its approach, dealing with the issues addressed.

There is no other book which speaks with such wisdom.

The bible says; "A certain woman."

Was it a dark skin colored, or a light skin colored woman?

Was it a Japanese, or Chinese, was it a South American, or Canadian?

Certainly it was none of the above.

The woman addressed was an Israelite. She was a Hebrew.

A certain woman is what was said, giving more focus on the issue that existed in the woman and the impact it had on her. Later, we will see how the focus is shifted to the woman in relation to the condition's impact on her life.

How did this certain woman disease affect her relationship with God and others? The answer is at the end, with you realizing your own similar situation?

This certain woman was a Jewess.

The massage which the bible is bringing out is that, that "Certain Woman's" dilemma could have been anyone's.

There maybe were other women with that same physical condition.

The scripture, with this account, brings out a couple facts.

1. This happened to a woman. Not an aged or young. Not a literate or illiterate. Not a slim or fat. Not a light or dark skin. Not a rough, or smooth skin, but a certain woman.
2. This certain woman's issue has been, and still is a woman's experience/condition.
3. The third fact is that, despite one's physical setback, or condition, (other than death) there is the possibility of that condition becoming better, or remedied. We can say worse too.

There is a saying used when solving financial crimes, which goes like this; "Let's follow the money trail." I say let us follow the word.

The woman had an "issue of blood." She had a physical condition in her blood which was a treat to her life, and taking away many things from her.

She was not only affected physically, but emotionally, and psychologically.

She was affected socially and relationally.

Due to the sickness which she was suffering from, and according to the custom of the day, she was prohibited from associating with the rest of the larger population. This woman was considered unclean.

This individual was a severely bruised woman. She was hemorrhaging internally. And that was far worse than if her bleeding was externally. The bleeding was not visible to anyone, but herself, and therefore could not have been monitored.

In today's language, she was anemic, a condition which negatively affect a person's blood cells.

This woman was not just losing her blood, she was losing her life. For the life is in the blood. With her blood gone, she would have no life.

Can you imagine that in the midst of today's technology, this is the condition of your daughter; no, not your daughter, but your wife or equally loved one?

To complicate things, the end of her suffering was no where near in sight.

How old was this "certain woman"? That was not given to us of her. However, the bible declared, that she suffered from this particular disease for twelve years.

That tells us at least four things;

1. She had already passed the flower of her age (pre-procreation years).
2. This, which she has experienced for twelve years, was considered to be a long time suffering. The bible speaks of a quality of the Spirit, which is longsuffering, and can also be considered as patience. This woman's case was different. She was suffering long, for twelve years, from uncertainty, embarrassment, and most definitely fear.

3. Another fact is that, due to the disease, it was unlawful for her to be with the general population.
4. She was probably twenty-five years of age.

For the sake of identity, let us call this woman "Janet Does".

Janet Does' physical condition denied her the God given privilege to be in the company of other people.

She was a lonely, very lonely woman. Society did not offer much to her, and whatever little she had was quickly disappearing. The people she knew had already taken everything from her. The only thing that remained between her and death was time. That too was fading.

Most of her friends, if not all, were no where to be seen. They were gone.

It is assumed that due to her affliction and the length of time afflicted, she was in great financial debt. Something she saw no easy way of repaying.

She maybe decided to with-hold paying her taxes, so that she could have paid her medical bills. Even those from whom she borrowed had no idea when they were going to be repaid.

The insurance companies in those days may have felt she was costing them too much, so they cancelled her policy.

What's even worse, her children is assumed, abandoned her, because she was draining their already small financial resources.

Have you ever felt that way, or know of anyone who went through, or is still in that position?

Janet Does experience brings me to an Old Testament passage of scripture 1kings 17:8-16; which speaks of God sustaining His servant Elijah, and at the same time taking care of, and supplying the needs of His daughter.

Chapter Three

He Did It Before

The Spirit of the LORD spoke unto Elijah saying; "Arise, get thee to Zarephath, which belongeth to Zidon, dwell there; Behold, I have commanded a widow woman there to sustain thee." 1Kings 17:9

With that declaration, Elijah had much confidence and faith in his God that he would be taken care of.

"So he arose, and went to Zarephath, and when he came to the gate of the city, behold, the widow woman was there gathering of sticks, and he called to her and said; Fetch me, I pray thee, a little water in a vessel that I may drink." 1Kings 17:10

These two people, Elijah, and the widow woman, both had a few things in common.

1. They were both affected by the drought.
2. They both needed each other, even unknowingly.
3. They were both hungry. The need of the flesh came upon them.
4. They both needed the same person, the LORD God.
5. Their needs were met at the same time.

Out of that which appeared to be negative and bad, (the drought) the Omnipotent God brought something good from it.

He brought increased blessing, Joy, satisfaction, and contentment.

"And as she was going to fetch it, he called to her, and said. Bring me, I pray thee, a morsel of bread in thine hand.

And she said; As the LORD thy God liveth, I have not a cake, but a handful of meal in a barrel, and a little oil in a cruse; Behold, I am gathering two sticks that I may go and dress it for me and my son, that we may eat it and die.

And Elijah said unto her; Fear not, go and do as thou hast said, but make me thereof a little cake first, and bring it unto me and after make for thee and thy son.

For thus saith the LORD God of Israel; "The barrel of meal shall not waste, neither shall the cruse of oil fail, until the day that the LORD sendeth rain upon the earth.

And she went and did according to the saying of Elijah, and she, and he, and her house did eat many days.

And the barrel of meal wasted not, neither did the cruse of oil fail, according to the word of the LORD which He spoke by Elijah." 1Kings 17:15

What an amazing experience this widow woman had.

Trust; Confidence in God.

Hope; Looking forward to, or having the expectation for something.
Humility; Absence of pride.
Hospitality; Cordial and generous reception of guests.
Faith; Not doubting, not wavering.

The circumstance surrounding that event was fear, worry, even starvation and death.

The land was going through a period of drought, severe drought. One where there was no rain for a couple of years, and the uncertainty of not knowing when the rain was going to eventually start pouring upon the land.

This drought was so severe, that even the man of God was feeling the brunch of the effect which came along with it.

He was feeling the same effect because he was a human being.

He was feeling the same effect because he should have stored up when there was plenty.

Elijah felt the effects of the drought, because he was human as everyone else.

He felt the effects because he too, had the same needs as his neighbor.

Why will one think, or even believe that the declining economic state of the country, and our world by extension; the economy is not negatively affecting the men and women of God?

Did you get that? Let me put it this was.

The global impact of a country's economy does not exempt anyone from its infringement. Not even the man/woman of God.

None is immune. Only the dead is.

It is trust and faith in God almighty that keeps, and sustains. With such faith and trust in Him, He will provide.

Elijah! Arise and go to Zarephath, a place in Zidon.

Zidon is the alternate to Sidon, and is of the territory of the Canaanites.

When you get there, someone will take care of you. I have already spoken to the person, commanding, that you be taken care of.

It is interesting, and sometimes unfair to the natural mind, considering the ones God chooses to carry out great roles. Of all the people from whom the LORD God had to choose, He chose a widow.

God wanted to show that He can be depended on, not only in plenty, but in lack also. He did not want to choose someone who had, but rather someone who had a need to be met. Someone who was vulnerable to the economic condition which everyone was experiencing.

Definitely, you and I would not have made that kind of choice.

In today's society, and with so much technology available to us, we definitely will search out for persons like Mr. Gates, and the queen of TV talk show host. We certainly will not consider going to a grieving widow. Compassion has a great role in making such a decision.

Here are some possible expectations we can experience from a widow.

a) She no longer had a bread-winner.
b) She lacked the comfort, and sense of security having a husband gives.
c) She was still grieving over the passing of her husband.
d) She did not have anyone to do the manly duties in, and around the home.
e) She did not have a big enough family to rely on who can give her support, and comfort.

Through the natural eyes, we see two people being seriously affected by the famine which was obviously brought on by the drought. Those two people, Elijah, the man Prophet of God, and the widow had the same thing in common. The LORD God used her to sustain him, and at the same time sustained her through him. They were both used by God to be an avenue of blessing to each other. How amazing!

Abraham would have been much better off, if only he had walked in the same spirit as this widow woman. Life among the Jews and Arabs today would have been different. Certainly, life in that part of the world, and among the Jews would have been more peaceful.

Due to the famine in Canaan of Abraham's day, and without seeking God's council, and direction, he went down into Egypt. That decision played out very negatively in his life, both domestically and relationally.

We know of the account very well, I hope.

Abraham made a grave mistake which involved, and affected, not only himself, but his family. For fear of dying, he denounced his wife Sarah before the king of Egypt. That which Abraham did was several years later repeated in the life of his son Isaac. The account you will find in Genesis 12:10-19, 20:1-11, and 26:1-11.

How did Elijah introduced himself to this [seemingly hopeless] widow woman is left to be known. However, the bible said that as he got to the gate of the city, he saw the woman gathering sticks [something which could have been found any where and everywhere due to the dryness of the land] and he called out to her.

"Fetch me, I pray thee a little water in a vessel that I may drink." 1Kings 15:10(b)

What a way to address or make a request to a stranger, or anyone for that matter. Imagine that being you, would he have gotten away with that in today's society, I think certainly not.

Did she know, or knew not who this man was, or was she acquainted with him?

Opinions may differ, but it is believed she knew who he was. She also knew whom he represented. Verse twelve of 1kings

17 alluded to that. And she said; "As the LORD thy God liveth, I have not a cake, but a handful of meal in a barrel, and a little oil in a cruse, and behold, I am gathering two sticks, that I may go in and dress for me and my son, that we may eat it and die."

According to the text, the woman complied with the man of God request. This here too, suggested that she knew who he was, taking into consideration her desperation and outstanding need.

As she went, he called out to her saying; "Bring me, I pray thee a morsel [small piece; not much. There was not much to give from anyway] of bread in thine hand.

I can imagine this woman as she stopped in her tracks for a couple of seconds, in shock and dismay, was about to ask; did I hear what I think I heard you say? Which was certainly going to be followed up with the next question; thou man of God, where is your mercy, where is your heart? I am a widow, still grieving over my husband's death, and having no one else to provide for me.

However, before any of this could have been said, she thought carefully; and as James said; "Let every man be swift to hear, slow to speak, slow to wrath." James 1:19(b).

This widow woman exercised that principle. Many folks today would have had to repent after such demands are made on them.

However, she said; "As the LORD thy God liveth, [so she knew who he was] I have not a cake [I do not have what you are asking for] but a handful of meal in a barrel [when I last saw], and a little oil in a cruse [small jar used for holding water]. 1Kings 17:12(a) When you entered the gates and saw me gathering sticks, I was about to go and use it for me and my son, that we may eat the last of it and die, because there will be no more left for us to feed on. 1Kings 17:12(b)

That is all fine, and okay; "Fear not, go and do just as you have said, and intended; however, make me thereof a little cake first."1Kings 17:13

I can hear him speaking as if he was the woman's father, if not husband.

Her compliance to the man of God request was important for her deliverance and sustenance.

Ultimately, her blessing depended on the word, "first." What she did first was crucial to her, and her son's survival.

Is not this the same principle our LORD God is asking of us His children, that we give to Him first? It certainly is:

I. The first-fruit
II. The first tenth
III. Love Him first, and above all else
IV. Seek ye first the kingdom of God and His righteousness.

Many today, being faced with the same or similar situation would have missed the blessing, and therefore would have died due to the famine. No, not the famine, but their lack of faith during the time of lack.

How often do we meet people while going about our business, and ignore their request to having their needs met? Before seriously assessing the situation to determine what is best, we make known our refusal.

From our kitchen window we view our neighbor strolling across the lawn to our house and before knowing the reason, it was already decided in our mind he/she is seeking to have something borrowed again. Our answer is already in the negative. The reason being, we have already switched into judgmental mode.

The wise man Solomon said; "He who answers a matter before hearing it, it is a folly and shame unto him." Proverbs 18:13

We did not properly assess the person's need. To you, he/she looked homeless, one who has contracted a disease, or maybe looking for someone, from whom they can get some drugs.

No; Maybe not that. He looked like a sex-offender, searching for someone to prey upon. Maybe, not even that. However; whatever the circumstance, the same judgment is passed on him/her as was done by everyone who passed before you. You gave to him the same as the others, judgment.

The apostle Paul in his letter addressed to the Romans said; "If thine enemy hunger, feed him; if he thirst, give him drink, for in so doing thou shalt heap coals of fire on his head" Rom. 12:20

Is he not the man they said stole all the Church's money? Now, here he is on the street molesting everybody. This is the way you look at, and therefore, see many people today. People we do not know, and with whom we are not even acquainted.

It is believed that people who are walking in the Spirit, and therefore being lead by the same Spirit (the Spirit of God) will not fear, but do their God-assigned responsibility in their service to His calling upon their lives.

Coming to mind is Peter and John response to a request made, which is recorded in the book of Acts 3:1-6, while on their way into the temple, they came to a beggar at the gates. Upon seeing Peter and John about to go into the temple, made his most heard request; "asked an alm," Acts 3:3. But Peter, fastening his eyes on him said; "Look on us." Acts 3:4

One may think that act by Peter was hypnosis, but it was not. Hypnosis, according to the "American Heritage Dictionary", is an artificially induced sleeplike condition, in which the individual is extremely responsive to suggestions made by the hypnotist. They sought to have the beggar's full attention so that he was not distracted by the many people entering in and out of the temple. For all of his life he saw each individual as an opportunity to have his need met, and with Peter and John taking up his attention, to him would have seem to be lost opportunities.

They did not have what the beggar was asking for, but he got what they had.

"Silver and gold, they said, have I none, but such as I have give I thee; in the name of Jesus Christ of Nazareth rise up and walk." Acts 3:6

They had Jesus, they had Joy, they had salvation, and they had power.

What did that beggar man got? He got Jesus, Joy, Salvation, and Power. Even his disability was taken care of. He no longer depended on others, but on his independence.

The man is believed, lived happily thereafter.

This too, reminds me of a passage in the gospel of Matthew 6:33, which reads; "Seek ye first the kingdom of God and His righteousness, and all these things shall be added unto you."

Based on that scripture; is it not true that the children of God are to seek God's Kingdom first, after which their needs are going to be met?

The prophet Elijah is believed to have understood the principle of being blessed, which is found in sowing and reaping, giving and receiving.

"Give and it shall be given unto you, good measure, pressed down, and shaken together, and running over shall men give into your bosom. For with the same measure that you mete withal it shall be measured to you again." Luke 6:38

That is also understood to mean; if you fail to give willingly, and voluntarily; in return, you will have nothing to receive. That is the principle of sowing and harvesting.

Not only Elijah knew the principle of being blessed, but also the widow. She went and did according to the request of the man of God. Her action resulted in Elijah, herself, and her son having bread to eat for many days. Even the land got its portion. The rain came and the land was able to produce food again.

It was the apostle Paul who said in Philippians 4:19; "But my God shall supply all your needs (not some, but all) according to His riches in glory by Christ Jesus."

The Philippians sowed into the Apostle Paul's life and ministry.

Chapter Four

The Road Of Uncertainty

Twelve years is considered a long time to be suffering. By then, many would have lost hope of recovery. Many would have grown accustom to the feeling. The condition would have now become the person's twin.

The advertisement might have been placed for an assistant to help end the misery of suffering. I remember a certain doctor who, some years ago was incarcerated for assisting sick patients with the termination of their lives.

To many, the will to live would have been absorbed in the twelve years of suffering, affliction, and isolation from family, friends, and the greater population. Somehow, that was not the case with that afflicted woman. She already had some experience, and therefore knew the joy of living and enjoying it to the fullest. Maybe, she had just entered her thirties and was anticipating a full life ahead of her. Her eyes were set on what is today's Hollywood. She, possibly had several big dreams, a couple of them was, winning the Grammy awards.

The issue; her issue, at first did not appear to be a problem. This will soon pass, she might have said. It's just the usual monthly ladies cycle. With regards to some local treatments for certain types of painful discomfort, some people might be experiencing, they would conclude, that is a "gas pain." The gas is bothering me, they will say, and as such, consume that which they think, or believe will take care of the so-call gas pain. They will feel the same way for days, and they will continue to treat the pain the same way, by ingesting the same thing which they have been, for days earlier. Their notion is that it will soon go away. The pain, from their assumption is in the same area of the body as the last one has been. Not knowing, this time it is not the same pain.

Gas is blamed for what is soon to be a massive heart attack. Is not that a scaring thing to you? To me, it is. That which was first considered to be just the usual woman's monthly cycle, has now become a continuous hemorrhaging. She started postponing some of her appointments. She even began staying in bed for longer periods of time, and when she did left the house, it was later than she usually would. Her schedules were all changing, which caused her life to take a different turn.

She began to lose track of the day, and its time.

As the days passed, and losing wages, she decided to make some new appointments. One of which was to visit her Primary Care Physician (PCP).

Blood sample was taken, and tests done.

Prescriptions were written, medications bought, and taken with no sign of relief, or the stoppage of her hemorrhaging.

In her desperation, she was referred to one physician after another.

The bible says; She suffered (went through) numerable things of numerable physicians.

There was no physician whom she did not know, and every physician knew of her condition. She visited those who worked under the light, and those who worked in the dark. Those who were licensed to practice their craft and those who were not licensed to practice. She saw everyone who offered her help, even those who used the colored candles behind the curtain in the dark of the night.

In the process of seeing and meeting one physician after another, she spent everything that she possessed.

It is believed that, when her money was finished, she sold most of her material belongings to pay her debt, and medical bills. Was her spending an act of faith, or one of desperation? Was she acting out of fear of dying, or fear of not accomplishing her dreams? What ever was the cause, she spent it all.

I looked at this woman, whom we identify as Janet Does, and I see not only a sick and desperate person. I see also an angry woman filled with loneliness. She once trusted in her accumulated wealth, and relied heavily on her insurance policy. To her then, God and His salvation did not matter, one way or another. She had no time for God. Too busy making the dough (a down to earth term for money). She worked different jobs, because of her big dreams and plans for life. She was on the road to fame and success. In today's society, Hollywood makes them a singing sensation before they get to age twenty. Just before they get to thirty, they would have gone into rehab twice. They have become addicts, and ill-disciplined, disrespectful to all forms of authority.

There were many men visiting the area. Those who were there on business, and those who were not on business, but vacationing. There were those who were just passing through, visiting friends and family. They all noticed her beauty, and charm. She made her looks flattering to them, and they desired a taste of what she was offering.

The wise man, Solomon was caught in such a snare. At the ending of his road, he penned these words to the others following; "My son; keep my words, and lay up my commandments with thee. Bind them upon thy fingers; write them upon the table of thine heart. That they may keep thee from the strange woman; from the stranger which flattereth with her words. For at the window of my house, I looked through my casement, and beheld among the simple ones (unsuspecting), I discerned among the youths, a young man void of understanding (not knowing).

Passing through the street near a corner, and he went to the way to her house.

In the twilight, in the evening, in the black and dark night;

And, behold, there met him a woman with the attire of a harlot, and subtle of heart. She is loud and stubborn; her feet abide not in her house. She in now in the streets, and lieth in wait at every corner. So she caught him, and kissed him, and with an impudent (immodest behavior) face said unto him. I have decked my bed with coverings of tapestry, with carved works, with fine linen of Egypt. I have perfumed my bed with myrrh, aloes, and cinnamon. Come, let us take our fill of love until the morning; let us solace (to comfort) ourselves with loves. With her much fear (subtle) speech, she caused him to yield; with the flattering of her lips she forced him. He goeth after her straightway as an Ox goeth to the slaughter, or as a fool to the correction of the stocks. Till a dart strike through his liver; as a bird hasteth to the snare, and knew not that it is for his life. For she has cast down many wounded; yes, many strong men have been slain by her. Her house is the way to hell, going down to the chambers of death." Proverbs 7:1; 3; 5 & 6; 8-13; 16-18; 21-23; 26-27.

There are many in our society whose lifestyle fit the above. And that too, could have been Janet Does. However, the bible made no such statement of her. That would have been her real problem.

This is what the bible says in the book of John 4:7-42. This is more than half the chapter which has fifty four verses.

Reference will be made to a few of the verses within the passage given.

One day Jesus was travelling from one place to another. Between those two places, He came to a well where He stopped for a moment to rest. Suddenly there came a woman of Samaria to the well to draw water (as she did everyday). A conversation developed between both of them. The woman's adult life story was unfolded to her by Jesus.

As we all know, many conversations do not end on the note they began. So was Jesus' with the woman at the well.

In the course of their conversation, there came the time when Jesus requested that she go and call her husband, and that she should return with him. John 4:16.

Her response to His request was; I do not have a husband.

Jesus commended her for her truthfulness, and further told her that she currently had five husbands who were not hers. They belonged to other wives. She was, at that time engaged in intimate relationships with five men, none of which was her husband. The frightening truth was that, none of the five men knew of her relationship with the others. She was a professional, and seemed to have had a degree in that lifestyle. That day, the Samaritan woman, whom all others saw as the worse, and obviously, the most destructive person around, became the most influential person, not just woman, but person, in all of Samaria. She became the greatest evangelist of the land. God can, and indeed take that which man condemns and use for His glory. Men counted her out, but Jesus Christ counted her in. Men wiped her off to be anything good, but Christ wiped away sins, and made something good out of her. Men wiped away her name from among them, but Christ gave her a name with Him. Their behavior to her was similar to that of the condemned thief who was left to die on the cross next to Jesus. They both also had similar experience with Jesus Christ. They met someone who loved and cared for them, they were saved.

Men provided water that when she drank, did thirst again, but Christ gave unto her water which she drank and was filled.

Her people took away her peace, but Christ restored it unto her. They may have identified, and described her by many different names, but Jesus called, and identified her by one; "Woman." John 4:21

Now, keep in your mind, the woman with the issue of blood.

It is proven and known that women who go around having sexual relationships with men, and at the same time, unprotected, do contract sexually transmitted disease (STD), which in turn is passed on to others with whom she has sexual intercourse. That behavior, of course goes both ways. Some of them were, and are diagnosed with ovarian cancer, and of course, die from the disease. The woman who is afflicted with ovarian cancer sometimes experiences a continuous flow of blood more frequently, and sometimes between menstrual periods, more than, and over an extended period of time, more than those who do not suffer with such a condition.

It can only be imagined by someone who does not have that experience, how uncomfortable and embarrassing such condition can make one to feel.

The woman with the issue of blood was believed to be suffering from a similar condition. In her day, there was no radiation instrument except for the sunlight. There was no one to do surgery as there is today.

There most-likely were the "bush doctors," the "witch doctors," the "know it best" doctors, and certainly the "medically trained doctors," though the medical science was not as advanced as we have it today. Despite the advancement in medical science now, more people are dying today of the same disease than in the days of the prophets, and of the early church in the time of Jesus Christ.

It is believed that many times over, more people are contracting the same disease, and obviously too, more deadly ones.

It is also important to note, that in both times (Jesus and now), there were those who were, and are being healed, or delivered from their disease. We see this through the use of medical treatment; not forgetting therapy and exercise (physical or otherwise), as well as faith in Jesus Christ.

There are those who are referred to the use of herbs
Of such people, was:

1. The centurion servant, according to the account given in Luke 7:2-10.
2. The ten lepers who are mentioned in Luke 17:11-19.
3. There is also the man who was bed-ridden with palsy, as mentioned in Mark 2:1-5.
4. What about the deaf and dumb. To the mind, and reasoning of some, this may not make much sense, if any at all (other than for the demonstration of the power of God) having ears, and cannot hear. I am inclined to believe that God, even though He is a great decorator, and beautician, did not put mans ears to the side of his head for beauty, or for balance. It was for hearing. The same applies to having a tongue, and cannot speak; even the eyes. Mark 9:25
5. The book of Mark 8:22-25, gives to us an account of a man who was blind, whom Jesus ministered unto by putting spit on his eyes so that his sight will be restored.

The functions of those two organs; parts of the body are to hear through the use of the ears, and speak through the use of the tongue.

6. To the extreme, we have the account of Lazarus the brother of Mary out of whom Jesus cast out demons, and Martha her sister. He was already dead and buried, days before experiencing deliverance from death. The account of this you will find in John 11. A similar situation is found in 2Kings 13:21, when a man was being buried in the sepulcher of the prophet Elisha. When they saw other men approaching, they let go of the dead man who eventually fell upon the already decomposed corpse of Elisha. That moment of fear and impulsive reaction by the pallbearers, resulted in the unexpected restoration to life of the dead man.
7. Many people do not expect much from a fisherman, but fish, and maybe swimming lessons. In the book of Acts 9:36-41, we are told of a situation where a woman named Dorcas was sick, and eventually died of her sickness. She was very charitable and much loved by all those who knew her. Many of the people in her and neighboring communities benefited from her skills and talent. This charitable and loved woman was from the town of Lydda. Lydda was a town ten miles south of Joppa where the Apostle Peter lived. The family of Dorcas, upon hearing that Peter was there, sent two men expressing their need, and that he should hasten and not delay. Getting to the place where the dead laid, he met everyone weeping and displaying to him some of the things which

Dorcas produced when she was alive. Peter, the man of God, put them all out of the room and kneeling down, prayed, turning to the body and said; "Tabitha! Arise". Dorcas, who was dead, opened her eyes and sat up. She was then lifted up to her feet by Peter who then presented her alive to her mourners and the people.

8. Was it not the Prophet Elisha who raised the Shunammite woman son back to life? The same woman whom he prophesied would have a child; 2Kings 4 speaks of the account. "About this time of season, according to the time of life, you shall embrace a son. And she said, no, my lord, thou man of God. Do not lie to thine handmaid. And the woman conceived, and bore a son at that season that Elisha had said unto her according to the time of life. And when the child was grown, it fell on a day that he went out to his father to the reapers. And he said unto his father; my head, my head. And he (the father) said to the lad, carry him to his mother. And when he had taken him and brought him to his mother, he sat on her knees till noon, and then died. And she went up, and laid him on the bed of the man of God, and shut the door upon him, and went out. 2Kings 4:16-21.
   "And when she came to the man of God to the hill, she caught him by the feet, but Gehazi came near to thrust her away, and the man of God said; "Let her alone, for her soul is vexed within her, and the LORD has hid it from me, and has not told me. Then she said; did I desire a son of my lord? Did I not say, do not deceive me? Then he said to Gehazi; Gird up thy loins,

> and take my staff in thine hand, and go thy way; if thou meet any man, salute him not, and if any salute thee, answer him not again, and lay my staff upon the face of the child. And the mother of the child said; As the LORD liveth, and as thy soul liveth, I will not leave thee. And he arose and followed her. And Gehazi passed on before them, and laid the staff upon the face of the child, but there was neither voice nor hearing. Wherefore he went again to meet him, and told him saying; "The child is not awake. When Elisha had come into the house the lad was already dead, and lying upon his bed. He went in therefore, and shut the door upon them twain and prayed unto the LORD. And he went up and laid upon the child and put his mouth upon his mouth and his eyes upon his eyes, and his hands upon his hands, and he stretched himself upon the child, and the flesh of the child waxed warm. Then he returned and walked in the house to and fro, and went up and stretched himself upon him, and the child sneezed seven times, and the child opened his eyes. And he called Gehazi and said, call this Shunammite. So he called her and when she came in unto him, he said; Take up thy son."2Kings 4:27-36

These are some of the many amazing experiences of healing and deliverances, even the raising back to life of the afflicted and suffering.

We know how relieved and elated people become when their loved one has been resuscitated. Outside of salvation, I do not know if there is a greater feeling.

I hear the Spirit of Almighty God saying in Exodus 4:11-12; "who has made man's mouth, or who made the dumb, or the deaf, or the seeing, or the blind? Have not I the LORD?

Now (not later) therefore, go and I will be with thy mouth, and teach thee what you shall say."

This is strongly supported by Jesus Christ in the gospel of Mark 16:15-18; saying; "Go ye into all the world and preach the gospel to every creature. He that believeth and is baptized shall be saved, but he that believeth not shall be damned. And these signs shall follow them that believe; in my name shall they cast out devils; they shall speak with new tongues. They shall take up serpents, and if they drink any deadly thing, it shall not hurt them. They shall lay hands on the sick, and they shall recover."

The manifestation of Jesus' declaration in the passage is hinged on two words, and our relationship to them. Those two words are "go", and "believe." Disobedience to those two instructions is to take the opposing side of God.

Stubbornness breathes rebellion, and rebellion breathes disobedience. Disobedience on the other hand breathes sin, and not only breathes sin, but it is sin.

To sin is to disrespect God.
To sin is to dishonor God.
To sin is to disregard God and His place in and over our lives.

Jesus Christ first said to, "go," and as you go, "believe."

The reason and the plan are in His hands, which work together. Those who have made Jesus Christ their savior, should realize that He is moving about in them, while they go about their daily lives and business.

Jesus, knowing that He walks about in individuals, will bring healing and deliverance to those in need as believers lay hands, when coming into contact with others as they do ministry for Jesus Christ. Mark 16:17—18

We do not see the healing that Jesus speaks of because of several reasons.

1. As believers, we do not believe. That sounds strange eh? I agree with you, but the statement is true. Many of us call ourselves believers, but what does Jesus Himself says about that?

2. Those who believe; do not go. Is that not disobedience? I think so, don't you agree?

3. If we believe, and go; we do not do. We do not do, because we are afraid of what the skeptics will say, even if they say nothing. We are afraid of how we will be looked at, even when they are looking with the hope of receiving. As believers, and ambassadors for Jesus, and the Kingdom of God need to do is live the life. Yes, live the life of Him who called and assigned us. That will certainly make it easier for anyone to receive what we have to offer. Living the life of Jesus Christ convinces people that we are real. If we

> fail to live the life, they will see us as fake, and will not trust us, nor what we are offering to them.

When did Jesus say others will be healed? When we lay hands on the sick.

The three "go", "believe," and "lay"; must come together in one agreement, if we are going to experience what Jesus Christ commissions.

When they are not working together in ministry for Him; how is that described? I'm listening!!!

I admire the spirit and faith of the man dying of palsy, and those who carried him. They all believed, and their faith was rewarded.

Palsy is a condition that puts its victim in a paralyze state, and will have them to need help from others.

There were no wheel chairs, except for cots, similar to the stretcher, to carry the sick man. There was no motorized ambulance, except those who carried sick folks around, like that man who was let down on the stretcher in the presence of Jesus.

The faith of these people resulted in a double benefit for the man. He was not only healed, but he was also delivered from his years of sin. There are several factors which contributed to this man's healing and deliverance.

1. He and those who carried him believed his condition was curable.

2. His faith was not in his insurance policy, because he had none.
3. He did not allow his set-back (dependence on others) to keep him at home as many people today do.
4. He appreciated having the support of others.

Many today are not healed, because of the wrong and unwise decision which they make. They chose to stay at home, rather than to be where their healing is going to show up.

Like the woman with the issue of blood, they trusted in their money to buy them the health which they need.

They chose to turn to their insurance company, rather then turn to Jesus Christ.

There are even those who deny the seriousness of their condition, and need to be healed.

The man with paralysis and his companions did not allow the physical and environmental conditions to deny him the deliverance he desired, and sought.

In today's generation, we stay away from the house of God whenever we feel like. We allow however we feel or think to be good reason for us not being in God's presence (fellowship with the saints at the time of worship). Of course, there are those whose jobs sometimes will keep them away, and such are the exception. We have built our own pharmacy, and become our own pharmacist. There is a pill for everything.

Faith is now become a choice. Something to switch on, and switch off at will.

Sorry, let me take the pleasure to disappoint you. Under such condition, faith does not work.

We take the temple of God (our bodies) and make it a chemical lab.

There is absolutely no one better able to understand the needs and functioning of the human body than He who created it. This is; The LORD God Almighty.

That being the truth; then trust Him today and be delivered of thy plague. Accept the challenge that your mountain offers, and defeat it by your faith in the Lord Jesus Christ.

Chapter Five

Only By Faith

There are, at least four things we know of Janet Does (the woman with the issue of blood) prior to her meeting Jesus.

1. She had a sickness.
2. She had some wealth.
3. The affliction and suffering were upon her for at least twelve years.
4. She was acquainted with all of the practicing physicians in her day.

During the twelve years, Janet Does lost much, a couple of which was her wealth and her health. She went through disappointment after disappointment. Her friends became fewer, and fewer. Physically, her strength was failing with each passing day. Her appetite for food may have also been failing. The thing which kept her going was the desire to live. She was not ready to die; neither did she want to continue living in her condition.

The bible says; "she suffered (not few things, but) many things of (not her Primary Care Physician only, but) many physicians. Every one of them was familiar with, and knew of her condition. She went to doctor after doctor, and was recommended to many specialists. She continued to suffer, not only of her sickness, but from her many disappointments in being let down by all whom she met.

This woman, in my opinion was strong, both physically and mentally. She managed her twelve years of physical and emotional suffering very well.

I do not know how the health system worked in those days. However, I can safely say that the people then, had great faith.

In my head is a pretty good idea of what the system is like today. Certainly, as one will say, much to be desired.

It is the assumption that much financial resources passes through the system, justly and unjustly. Just to elaborate on that statement for a moment.

There are those who will disagree, and there are those who will agree.

Individuals who have committed premeditated crimes and have been caught, tried, and convicted for the crimes which they have committed, have (maybe) unknowingly to them, given up some of the freedom they had before the committing of those crimes. This mean, they do not possess the right, or have access to certain things as do the free society. Contrary to that, they make demand to the authorities that they under-go certain surgical procedures; eg, sex-change, otherwise called; "Gender Re-assignment Surgery," and that the same society whom they have offended with their crimes, bear the cost of those procedures.

They seek to have others finance changes to their sexual origin. He does not want to be a male anymore, so he uses his influence, and "constitutional rights" to have tax payers finance their lustful desires and ambitions.

In the days of Janet Does, medical surgeons were not as equipped to perform the necessary practice. There were not many pharmacists.

Whoever they were in the field of medicine, she knew them all.

In the physician's hands, was her bank account which had no money.

Fortunately for her, Jesus Christ was in her area as she was on her way to keeping another of her usual appointments.

Words reached her of Jesus' presence. Hearing such good news, hope sprang forth in her as her spirit was energized.

Her faith came alive. She had (in my opinion) great faith, considering her many years of suffering, with disappointing experiences. That was a mountain she had to, and eventually did over come.

Jesus said in the book of Matthew 17:20, "If you have faith as a grain of mustard seed, you shall say unto this mountain (which might and can be an addiction to illegal substance, or low self-esteem. It may be lustful desires that are plaguing you. What about the mountain of gambling uncontrollably). "This mountain", it was said can be anything that is preventing one from growing in their walk and relationship with Jesus Christ. "—remove hence (from before you, from your presence) to yonder place, and it shall (not maybe, not might, not I think, but shall) remove.

He did not stop there, but went on to say; "and nothing shall be impossible unto you."

Do you not remember when God created man (Adam) giving unto him dominion, power, authority, ruler-ship over the earth? Adam relinquished all those, but Jesus today, is seeking to restore all that which Adam gave up.

In scripture, we are told of a man who was widely known, and greatly loved. His name was Naaman. This man was afflicted with a rare sickness, of which he was to be pronounced unclean, and be isolated from the larger community.

He did not only have a sickness, but a mountain to overcome, if he was going to experience healing in his body, and be pronounced clean.

The name of that sickness was Leprosy, and the name of the mountain was Pride.

It is important to mention that, Pride in not just a feeling, or a behavioral trait.

It is more than that; Pride is a spirit which rules the heart, and controls the life it possessed. Pride is seen in the quality of life people exhibit. This will be elaborated on in a later chapter. If Pride controls your life, then you are certain to forfeit all of life's promises through Jesus Christ.

Naaman almost forfeited his healing.

The bible states that Naaman was a captain in the Syrian army. At the time of his sickness, the Syrian army fought against Israel, and captured some of their people. Among those captured was a young girl, who eventually became maid to Naaman's wife. She being in Naaman's home, heard of his condition. She then said to her mistress; "would God my lord (Naaman) were with the prophet that is in Samaria, for he will recover (heal) him of his leprosy." 2Kings 5:3

At the time of this event, Samaria was the capital of Israel. Today the capital is Jerusalem.

The nation of Israel, as we know it today, was a divided kingdom in the times of the prophets.

The northern kingdom, was Israel, and the southern, Judah. This is no longer the situation, she (Israel) is now established as one kingdom.

Naaman was informed of the maid's conversation with his wife concerning him being healed. Hearing that, he became hopeful. He then made arrangements to visit Israel to see the man of God, Elisha. As Naaman and his travelling staff got to Samaria, and came to Elisha's house, they stood at the door, expecting to be greeted by Elisha. However, Elisha knowing that he had visitors, and the purpose of their visit, sent his servant unto Naaman saying; "go and wash in Jordan seven times, and thy flesh shall come again to thee, and thou shall be clean."

It could have been very amusing hearing Naaman's response.

What! Did I hear correctly? Does he really mean for me to do that? I wonder if that prophet, whatever his name is; know who I am?

All those possible questions went through Naaman'a mind, when he finally asked; "are not Abana, and Pharpar, rivers of Damascus (Damascus was the chief city of Syria), better than all the waters of Israel, may I not wash in them and be clean?" 2Kings 5:2

Naaman, who was filled with Pride, felt disrespected, insulted, and humiliated.

What did he do? He walked away.

Elisha already knew that Naaman' continuous condition was the result of the mountain he built up in his own life. To be healed, he first had to demolish the mountain. No one else could have done it for him.

Pride being a condition of the heart which is reflected through the life lived, was targeted by Elisha the prophet.

Naaman's healing was hinged on humility (he humbling himself), so Elisha gave him the challenge. He, at first blew it, but thank God for his staff who convinced him, and he got another opportunity. He received healing after his mountain was demolished. Naaman's deliverance was always dependant on himself, but he did not realize it.

The same spirit which possessed Naaman, walks in and out of churches today. It walks in and out of doctors offices. Too many people walk away from their deliverance and healing.

They prefer to remain stuck-up on the mountain of pride, than be free of the burden of dying in their condition.

Naaman became very angry and went away. Those who accompanied him on the trip felt disappointed in him for walking away. They, however, discouraged him from going without being healed, by saying to him; "my father, if the prophet had bid thee to do some great thing, would you not have done it, how much rather then, when he say to thee, wash, and be clean?" 2Kings 5:13

With that said, the spirit of pride (in the language of the boxing sport) received a blow beneath the belt, which caused it to go down. The Syrian general experienced deliverance from the spirit of Pride. Naaman turned around, went, and dipped his unclean and once proud self seven times in the Jordan River.

1samuel 15:22 says; "to obey is better than sacrifice, and to hearken than the fat of rams."

Naaman, not only came out of the Jordan River cleansed of his leprosy. His mountain of Pride was left on the river bed. You too can be set free of that plague. You too can see you mountain vanish (disappear) from before your face.

You too can be relieved of that unnecessary burden.

There was a song-writer who said; "faith in God can move a mighty mountain. Faith in God can calm life's troubled sea. Have Faith in God."

It was the great evangelist, R.W. Schambach who said; "You don't have any trouble. All you need is faith in God."

Chapter Six

No More Shame

Jesus is the one who said; it is easier for a camel to go through the eye of a needle than for a rich man to enter into the kingdom of God. Mark 10:25

Most obvious, such individuals trust in the uncertainty of their riches. Trusting in the uncertainty of wealth can be very devastating to the one who do such.

Many have suffered, many are suffering, and many will suffer unnecessarily.

The experiences are before our eyes, of those who have gone through, and are still being rehabilitated to normalcy.

Having great wealth does not destroy, but one's trust in great wealth does.

The account is given in the bible of a young rich man who lived in Palestine during the time of Jesus Christ. Mark 10:17-25

This young man, it is believed has a great desire for eternal life, but found himself falling short of obtaining it.

The time came when he had the opportunity to enquire of Jesus what was it he needed to do.

Master! What shall I do that I may inherit eternal life? He asked.

In Jesus' response to the man's question, he first reminded him of that which he knew. Thou knowest the commandments; do not commit adultery. (There are many who believe, having money gives them the liberty to sleep with other people's wives or husbands. Take a peek at Hollywood. Some get married, divorce and remarry before a child enters grade school). Do not kill, do not steal. Do not be a false witness (nor encourage others to do so). Do not defraud others. Honor thy father and mother. Mark 10:25

Respect them. Now that you have become wealthy, do not step upon them.

The young man informed Jesus by saying; all that which you said should not be done, I have been observing, even from my youth.

This was a very successful business man who did not know what was hindering his Joy and happiness, until he met with Jesus.

He was well liked, and favored by those who knew him, though may not have known he had an inner emptiness.

He had the wealth, but felt empty. He had great riches, but felt naked. He had all that there was to eat, but remained hungry.

Jesus, who knew the man's pain, turned to him and said; one thing you lack, go thy way and sell whatsoever you have and give to the poor, and you shall have treasure in heaven. Mk. 10:21

To the natural and human mind, those surely are not encouraging words.

Is Jesus saying to me the reader to give away all of my wealth? Is he saying to me to sell all that which I possess, and distribute the proceeds to the poor? Absolutely not! That is not what the good master is saying.

Jesus realized that the young man had in his possession everything he materially needed, but was not happy.

What Jesus also realized, was that the young man was seeking for happiness all of his adult life and was unable of obtaining it. His riches and popularity were big hindrances to the happiness he sought for.

His wealth and fame were road blocks between him and eternal life.

If by your great wealth, you possess the joy and happiness that you need, then it is needless that you sell off all that you have and give to the poor. If by your significant wealth you do not possess an inner emptiness, then there is no need for you to sell off that which you have in search of fulfillment. That, in essence is what Jesus was saying to the young man.

On another occasion, and at a time of addressing greed, Jesus said; a man's life does not consist in the abundance of the things which he/she possess. Luke 12:15

Trust not in oppression, and become not vain in robbery. If riches increase, set not your heart upon them. Psalm 62:10

It is good to be wealthy; however, there should be a right relationship between one-self, other people, and the substantial wealth he/she has.

The general epistle of 3 John 2, he declared; "beloved, I wish above all things that thou prosper and be in good health, even as thy soul prospereth."

Being materially prosperous is not against the will of God. However, according to the scripture you have just read, and others, one's material prosperity and strength should not have precedence to the growth and strength of the soul.

The gospel of Luke 7, gives a detailed account of a woman, who seemingly trusted in the abundance of her wealth, and struggled with emptiness until she met Jesus.

This was not Mary, of whom so much is known. Neither was it Janet.

She was a woman of the city of Capernaum, who was disliked by the residents of her village and surrounding neighborhood.

Capernaum is a city on the shore of Galilee which was frequented by Jesus in his travels.

Many of his miracles were done here and experienced by multitudes of followers.

This woman, who is described as sinner, was very wealthy.

Without invitation, she intruded the home of a very respectable city official who was a Pharisee.

She, going into this Pharisee's home uninvited, was not unusual for one to do in the time and ministry of Christ. Where ever Jesus went, everyone else invited themselves.

This woman, who was so well known by her village and town's residents, could have been accused of stealing. In her possession in the Pharisee's house was an alabaster box of ointment.

Alabaster was a rare and precious translucent stone, used to make decorative things.

Does diamond comes to mind? I thought so.

This box of ointment was of significant value, which could have been some of the proceeds of her sin.

The focus of attention in the home of the Pharisee was no longer on Jesus' presence there, but on this very disliked, and sinful woman.

Maybe she had no intention of stopping Jesus from attending to his host. She maybe was too ashamed to do so, and being the person she was would have seen that as disrespectful. She stood behind Jesus, and weeping helplessly, stooped and began to wash his feet with her tears.

To many, she was seen as the worst, and made to feel so. As you read, and reflecting on your past, you see some similarity of this woman in your life. You can relate to some of the things, and the shame she could have been experiencing.

She, who knew herself better than all of her accusers, was most repentant.

The Pharisee, in whose house Jesus was visiting, had been hoping to become more famous among his peers.

His rating was expected, he thought would have gone up by thirty points. This woman however, was not looking for recognition or rating. She was worshipping, and seeking forgiveness from Jesus.

A woman's hair brings out her beauty. This sinful woman was not concerned about her beauty. She was concerned about the emptiness of her soul. She wanted that which none of the men she has been with possessed. She lived an empty, unfulfilled and dissatisfied life, and was tired of it.

In a state where beauty was not her concern anymore, she wiped the feet of Jesus with the hairs of her head.

In desperate moments, people do desperate things.

This desperate woman now saw in Jesus that which no one else saw. She saw him being worthy to be treated as a king, and therefore treated him as such.

She publicly kissed Jesus' feet, after which she used her most precious ointment and anointed his feet.

Jesus' host by now, Simon the Pharisee, was not displeased with the woman only. He became critical of Jesus also.

To him, Jesus should have known who this woman is and her reputation, and therefore should not have tolerated her behavior, which seemingly was highly disrespectful.

Jesus, knowing Simon's thoughts, said to him after seeking permission, obviously, he was his host.

There was a certain creditor which had two debtors. One owed him five hundred pence, and the other owed fifty pence. When they were unable to pay (they both had nothing), he forgave them both. Tell me therefore, Jesus asked; which of the two will love the creditor most?

Simon's response; I suppose that he, to whom he forgave most.

The lesson Jesus was bringing out here is not to be passed over. It should not go unnoticed.

While Simon and others were very critical of the woman, and eventually Jesus in him neglecting the purpose for the invitation, he became more concerned about a sinner woman.

Jesus was concerned about a soul being saved, while the Pharisee was more concerned about his rating among his peers. The Pharisee was more the self-centered, and self-righteous one, but the woman was seen by Jesus as having a right heart.

In the gospel of Mark 2:17, Jesus said; They that are whole have no need for a physician, but they that are sick, I came not to call the righteous, but sinners to repentance.

This woman definitely saw herself as a sinner, and therefore swallowed her pride and shame.

Unlike the woman at the well of Samaria, mentioned in John 4; did not have to go and witness to the men she slept around with. They were already witnesses of what Jesus did in her life. She trampled down her obstacles to forgiveness, and deliverance.

Simon! Here is one way in which you and I are different.

You care about yourself, and I care about others.

Simon! I came into thine and you gave me no water to wash my feet, but this woman has washed my feet with tears, and wiped them with the hairs of her head. You gave me no kiss, but this woman, since the time I came in has not ceased to kiss my feet. My head with oil you did not anoint, but she has anointed my feet with ointment.

In your eyes, and your fellows, she is a sinner and you righteous.

Jesus might have said; tell me Simon, you be the judge of this. Between you and the woman, who took care of me? Who showed kindness? To whom did it cost more?

For your information Simon, her sins which are many, are forgiven, for she loved much, and therefore gave much.

Chapter Seven

Moved Into Action

The book of James 2:20(b), states; "Faith without works is dead."

What James is saying in plain language, is that, faith and action goes together. For earlier in verse eighteen, he said; "thou hast faith, and I have works. Show me thy faith without thy works, and I will show thee my faith by my works."

According to the passage, it is correct to say; faith without action is useless.

Faith is a quality that is expressed through our action.

Janet Does, becoming hopeful, and with faith in Jesus; broke forth, and kicking the dust. As a horse pushed by its Jockey coming from the back to win the race, off she went.

"If I may, but touch His clothes, I shall become whole." I shall be set free of my twelve years of suffering. My misery definitely shall be over.

No one in the crowd, or in near proximity of the crowd, possessed more faith than Janet Does.

I have not seen anywhere prior to this moment, anyone with (crazy) faith as this sick, distressed, and frustrated woman.

Janet Does was certain she was going to experience deliverance from her twelve years old sickness. She was hoping to regain that many years of her lost joy.

It has not been recorded anywhere, in library, or in history books.

This has not been taught at seminars, or lectured in classrooms, even when someone visits the doctor, expecting to be helped; without first having the doctor's attention, and reason for their visit.

On many occasions in Jesus' ministry, when healing, and deliverance took place, He was told of the patient's need, after which He responded by bringing about the expected desire, and expectation of the seeker.

This badly sick woman had Doctor Jesus attending to her without Him getting her attention, neither did she sought, and get His attention.

That kind of faith is very seldom seen, or heard of, even in Christendom.

In the gospel, book of Luke 7:11-14, the account is given where Jesus visited a city called Nain. As He came near to the gate of the city, there was a dead man being carried out of the city to be buried. He was the only son of his mother.

It is almost unbearable that a mother, giving birth and guidance to her children, and some years later, having to bury them.

The dead man's mother could have been experiencing severe grief over the lost of her only son. Making it more difficult for her was the earlier passing of her husband. She was a widow.

The bible says; when the Lord saw her in her state of grief, He had compassion on her, and said to her; "weep not." Luke 7:13

He then came and touch the bier (those who carried the corpse out to be buried.) They stood still, and Jesus said to the corpse; "young man, I say unto thee; arise!" Luke 7:14

That young man and Lazarus had the same need. This was because they both had gone through the same experience. Only that Lazarus' condition at the time of being called forth from the grave was worse.

Did He say anything to Janet Does? Of course not! He did not have to.

What about Lazarus? Yes Lazarus of whom much is known, as mentioned in the book of John 11:1-46.

He too was sick, and as a result, died of his sickness.

Jesus was sought for by his sisters, Mary and Martha. However, Jesus did not get to their home in time, as they would have hoped. However, when Jesus eventually got there, Lazarus was already dead, and buried.

Now that Lazarus is dead, what can Jesus now do to help the situation, and stop the weeping and grieving? Healing was out of the question. Much more had to be done for them.

When Jesus got to His guests home, a conversation regarding Lazarus' sickness, and subsequent death, developed.

Words of accusation for causing Lazarus to die were thrown at Jesus.

Realizing how the conversation was proceeding, He asked to be taken to the place where he was buried.

Upon getting to the place of burial, Jesus instructed them to take away the stone which had the tomb sealed.

With that done, He prayed unto God saying; "Father, I thank thee that thou hast heard me, and I knew that thou hearest me always, but because of the people which stand by I said it, that they may believe that thou hast sent me." John 11:41-42

After speaking to the Father; Jesus lifted His voice saying; "Lazaruusss! Come forth." John 11:43. That was a command which Lazarus voluntarily obeyed.

Mark 10:46-51, gives the account of a man named Bartimaeus, who, one day was on the highway, a most popular used road side begging, when he learned that Jesus was passing by; He then, with a loud voice, cried out; "Jesuussss! Thou Son of David, have mercy on me." Mark 10:47

Could you imagine, this man who had a need, and making a desperate cry for help, was discouraged from doing so. He was told by many to hold his peace, and keep quiet. In other words; "mister; will you please shut your mouth."

It was believed by some that he was not upper-class enough to have Jesus' attention.

How concerned are we of those in need as they seek Jesus?

All they are asking of us is where, and how to find Jesus.

Seek ye the Lord while He may be found, call ye upon Him while He is near.

Were they a people with compassion? Then the question is asked, are we a people of compassion?

Rather than allowing himself to be discouraged, he cried even louder; "Thou son of David, have mercy on me." Mark 10:48

Do you want Jesus to have mercy on you?

Then lift up your voice, and cry unto Him as Bartimaeus did. When you get his attention as Bartimaeus did, your faith will be ignited.

He got Jesus' attention, so Jesus stood still, and commanded that the blind man be brought to Him.

As most, if not all doctors would ask the patient who visits them; "what can I do for you today, or how can I help you?"

Jesus asked; "what is it that you want me to do for you?" Mark 10:51

Bartimaeus responded by saying; "Lord, that I might receive my sight." Mark 10:51. Bartimaeus was definitely tired of a blind and unexcited life. Jesus, I want to be able to see like everyone else. From what I hear taking place around me on a daily basis, there are things I am missing out on.

Despite the discouraging words cast at him, this blind man remained focus on two things:

1. He knew his need, and therefore, remained focus on what it was.
2. He knew the one who could heal him (Jesus Christ) was present, so he kept his attention focused on Him until his need was met.

This man was not going to give up. He had no intention of being deterred. That was out of the question, and Jesus knew that.

Contrary to the blind man, we believe Jesus already knows what our need is, so we should not have to bring the matter to His attention more than two times.

To me, that is more than being short winded. It seems very much like pride.

We give up too easily, and too soon. We think that asking more than two times is not of faith. Let the devil know that is a lie, having excess fat on it, which he orchestrated.

Of those mentioned, Lazarus and blind Bartimeus, including others who were not referenced, Luke 13:11-13; John 5:5-8; Jesus was made aware of the needs of those seeking His attention regarding their situation of death, and blindness, and other afflictions contracted.

But, of the woman with the issue of blood, He did not have that same experience. She did not allow Him to have it of her.

Some months ago, a woman whom I know very well, was taken to one of the nation's reputable medical institution. The reason being; she was seriously attacked with a seizure.

I learned that, while she was there at the institution, multiple tests were done on her, seeking to determine the cause of the seizure.

If any test was not done, that was because the equipment was not yet manufactured, or not available.

Added to that, they could not give her medication, due to the fact that, they did not know what caused the seizure.

I understood that, at the time of her being discharged, she was visited by the institution's chief neurologist, who said to her that she is now epileptic, and will continue to be so for the rest of her physical life. She was told that she will now have (did you hear that? have) to be ingesting medication for the duration of her life; for something they did not know the cause.

The woman I am speaking of is my wife.

The devil told a lie, and he did not know that there were those who heard and knew that he lied, big time.

I refused to accept those words spoken over my wife's life. Had I done that, I would have been accepting it over my life too, and I was not ready to make that decision, nor ever going to make it.

I am sorry, but I was not going to allow those negative words to determine the course of my wife's life, neither mine.

No, not while Jesus Christ is alive and well.

Jesus is the one who governs our lives.

I remember it being said in the scripture; "When God be for you, who can be against you?" Rom. 8:31

Janet Does allowed the medical practitioners to dictate and govern her life to the point where the insurance company would have dropped her policy. Her retirement fund was already liquidated, and her saving account was showing zero balance.

Standing at my wife's bed side, and hearing what was being said to her, was not encouraging.

Medically, she could not have been helped, because the tests, from which it was hoped something would have been found, said otherwise.

That still, was not the worse of the episode.

Moments before she was discharged, the said neurologist prescribed three sets of medication that she will have to consume orally.

Thank God for the understanding, and the ability which He has given me.

Indeed, I was disappointed.

Yes, I did feel to say what I thought, but I kept my peace.

Why on earth will one prescribe medication to someone, for something they, from medical science and perspective do not know the cause? That is a perfect situation for much greater problems.

Medication should be intended to first work against, or combat the problem, which is the root cause. Not the effects of the problem.

Addressing the effects, and not the cause of the effects, in my opinion, is giving cause to the problem remaining, if not reoccurring and growing worse.

However, not all of them are. Some are manufactured to eliminate the result; for example, the pain and not the cause of the pain. Eliminating the pain does not necessarily eliminate the cause of the pain. That situation does not tell you what is taking place, whether the condition is growing better or worse.

Is not that frightening?

"If I can, but touch his clothes, I shall be whole."

Just to touch the clothes of Jesus was enough for her.

The only thing I know makes a person behaves in that manner is "crazy faith." She had some, and used it all up on Jesus.

Chapter Eight

Facing The Challenge

The crowd surrounding Jesus was large, and naturally, was growing larger. To have a personal encounter with Jesus was on several occasions seen as an impossible task, considering the size of the crowd which usually thronged Him.

That was not so for Janet Does. She accepted the challenge which was before her.

To penetrate that sea of people to get to Jesus was a huge task ahead of her. Comprising that sea of people were the hungry, the curious, his critics, and the hypocrites.

With that, she had to consider several other things;

a. The size of the crowd.
b. The spread of the crowd.
c. Jesus' position within the crowd.
d. How the crowd was shifting.
e. Most definitely, the most advantageous route of travel for her.

She drew up a plan, and with it, a strategy for implementation. Was her plan workable? Yes! Indeed it was.

Did it work? That we will see soon. Janet Does went off in what could have been, and eventually was her final quest for healing. Through the rugged terrain she went, with her strategy in motion, and plans unfolding. Then the unexpected suddenly appeared in her path. The crowd (her mountain) was growing even larger, and with that its trust was shifted to her direction. That new and unexpected shift changed everything in Janet's mind. Certainly, she did not see that one coming, and therefore could not have planned for it. One positive thing remained though; she was already on the path to challenging her obstacle. With that unforeseen set-back, Janet gave consideration to a couple thoughts. She questioned within herself; how shall I handle this now? How larger is this crowd (mountain) going to get before I reached my target? She had to make adjustments, and make them quick. There was no way for her knowing the answer to her concerns and fears.

The challenge was already great, and becoming even greater, when "Mr. Doubt" immediately stepped into her path. Before realizing her confrontation with Mr. Doubt, she found herself starring eye-ball to eye-ball with his friend, "Mrs. Discouragement."

Coming out of the dark shadows of her mountain was "lord hope," and his five children:

1. Lord hope (lower-case) who represented the merciless attack upon her character.
2. Intimidation, who represented timidity as brought on by the good health of the others.
3. Little, self-esteem, who represented the self destructive position she took upon herself.

4. Distraction, the one who was not able to maintain focus on the subject.
5. There was also little self-confidence, who was always comparing herself with others.
6. And of course, there was unbelief, who was not too noticeable, and maybe the most dangerous, and deadly of them all. That one trusted in the arm of flesh, and life's present circumstances.

This was a very difficult time for Janet Does. Discouragement does knock on the doors of the best of us, and Janet was of no exception.

It was the Holy Spirit speaking through the great apostle Paul, saying; "There has no temptation taken you, but such as is common to man; but God who is faithful will not allow you to be tempted above that which you are able to bear; however, will, with the temptation make a way of escape, that you will be able to bear it." 1Corinthians 10:13

Janet Does was facing her moments of mental confusion, when she heard the voice of an old time friend, Mr. Good Hope, whom she met some twelve years ago, he who noticed her in her persistence to penetrate the multitude of people.

Without distracting her, nor breaking her momentum, called out saying; "You can do it Janet. Do not be an obstacle in your own path to success."

I remember a similar situation to Janet Does. This occurred centuries earlier in the life of David, David who was anointed the second king of Israel. Before taking up leadership on the seat of the throne, he was pursued by his predecessor, King Saul, who sought to kill him. Not finding anywhere in Israel to hide himself, he took refuge in the camp of Israel's enemy. Israel's enemy then, was the Philistines; 1Samuel 29. Achish who had given David refuge, and found him to be a true friend and ally; one day said to David; "Surely as the Lord liveth, you have been upright (faithful, sincere, honest) with me; in your going out, and in your coming back in. I have not found evil, nor seen any sign of betrayal in you since the day of your coming to me unto this day. However, the lords (generals) do not favor you." 1Samuel 29:6

In short, David, you will have to return to the base.

David, on numerous occasions showed his gratitude, and thankfulness to Achish for giving to him, and his six hundred men refuge from Saul.

His service was no longer welcome, because of fear in the generals' mind that while in battle, David will turn against them.

Logically! That is a possibly. However, look at the positioning of the troops.

With the army of Israel, being lead by King Saul, approaching the Philistine army from the front, and at the rear of the Philistine's army, were David and his men. That layout placed the Philistines in a very vulnerable position, from the generals of the Philistine's army position.

The Philistines could have been made into a cheese, or for that matter a burger sandwich. No; a turkey sandwich might have been more satisfying. 1Samuel 29:1-4.

The lords of the Philistines were not going to take that risk. They were afraid David and his men were going to become disloyal to them.

David and his men were dismissed from the battle, and sent home to Ziklag.

Upon returning to base with his men, they soon realized that something terrible went wrong.

Their fears were confirmed when they learned that the Amalekites had invaded their town, and destroyed everything possible, burning it with fire, also taking their wives, and children captives.

When David and his men found out what had happened, they lifted their voice and wept until they had no more strength to weep.1Samuel 30:4.

They cried until their strength left them.

I have some understanding of how it feels to have your wife unlawfully taken away from you. A feeling which no loving, and, or caring husband welcomes.

As you and I have been, greatly distressed, so too was David.

David's, however, could have been worse, due to the fact that all the other people (his men) who were with him, and having their wives and children taken also, considered stoning him. He might have felt responsible for their huge loss.

Which day in your life can be worse than this one like David's?

When you are at rock bottom, and cannot go any lower, there is only one place left for you to go, and that is up, so start climbing.

David did just that.

Rather than allowing the current situation to consume him, and therefore becoming more distressed, he asked Abiather the priest, for the ephod.

The ephod was a garment, particularly worn by the high priest when he sought God.

David was one who had crazy faith. He broke moral laws, and in so doing, pleased God.

After dressing himself with the ephod, he went before God, enquiring whether or not he should pursue the Amalekites.

David asked the Lord two questions which were very important.

In today's society, God will be told what is being done, and then will be asked, what He thinks about it.

It is always better to follow the LORD, rather than going ahead of Him. He pays us big dividends when we follow.

David has a good word of advice for each of us on the subject of following.

He was a very humble person. One who all of us can learn from; providing we are willing to humble ourselves as we follow.

His two questions are;

1. "Shall I pursue after this troop?" 1Samuel 30:8
   Certainly! David, you shall pursue after them, the Lord said. 1Samuel 30:8
2. "Lord, shall I overtake them?" 1Samuel 30:8
   . Of course David! You shall overtake them. Not only overtake them, but also, you shall recover everything that was stolen from you. 1Samuel 30:8

I recall the words of a famous song writer saying, and I quote; "I went into the enemy's camp, and I took back what he stole from me, took back what he stole from me, took back what he stole from me.

I went into the enemy's camp, and I took back what he stole from me, he's under my feet, he's under my feet, Satan is under my feet." David quickly arose from the corner of distress, and discouragement, and having his request approved by the Lord, pursued after the Amalekites.

His mission was one hundred percent (100%) successful. God was in the details.

This is the same David, who throughout the book of Psalm; gives to us comforting, and encouraging words.

For example; "I sought the LORD, and He heard me, and delivered me from all (not some, or few, but all) my fears. This poor man cried, and the LORD heard him, and saved him out of all his troubles." Psalm 34:4 & 6.

There is no trouble which you might be in, that the LORD cannot deliver, or save you from.

Do you now have to be walking in and out of sin, as if your life depended on it? Absolutely not! It was the Holy Spirit again, through the great apostle Paul, who declared in the book of Romans 6:1-2; "What shall we say then, shall we continue in sin, that grace may abound? God forbid. How shall we, who are dead to sin, live any longer therein?"

All such consideration were met with strong opposition.

The Psalmist declared in 27:14; "Wait on the LORD. Be of good (strong, enduring) courage, and He shall strengthen thine heart. Wait, I say, on the LORD."

If we shall hear those words, we shall live, but if we hear them not, we shall suffer the consequences.

Believing in herself; her spirit suddenly became energized with super sonic power.

As the thickening crowd pressed against her trust forward, she lowered herself as a means of deflecting the pressure, avoiding loss of precious, and much needed time. That was a wise decision, which was very rewarding.

That strategy was a relief to her, and believing that she was not far away from the master, she said within her spirit; "If I could just touch His clothes, I shall be whole." Mark 5:28

This draws my attention to the gospel of John 5:2-9. The account is given of a man this time.

Long period of sickness does not plague one sex only, but both sexes.

This sick man was the very opposite of Janet Does. His name too, was not given.

You may believe twelve years is a long time to be in a terrible state.

This man's length of time in affliction was thirty-eight years.

What was his age? The scripture did not give that information.

For how long was he at the pool? Again, there is no record or information of that.

It should be safe to assume that, considering the condition of his sickness, as mentioned by him to Jesus; Jn. 5:7; "Sir, I have no man, that when the water is troubled (stirred-up) to put me into the pool.") He was brought to the pool by someone.

There seemingly was nothing he could have done to get healed. As close as he might have been to the pool, there was always someone who, when the water is stirred, will get into it before him, even when he was next in line.

You might have thought that Janet Does condition was bad, considering the duration of time she suffered. Then tell me, how will one describe this man's case.

There is no condition too serious for Jesus; that He cannot heal, or deliver from.

If according John 5:4; stepping into the troubled pool cured and relieved people of whatever disease they had, what about Him who created the water?

Your present condition does not have to be your future condition.

Your many years of being sick, does not mean you have to be sick throughout your old age, nor the rest of your time on earth.

Jesus is well able to relieve you of that burden.

Trust Him now for your deliverance. If you feel that you do not possess the kind of faith as Janet Does, ask Him to help you so that your faith can increase.

An example of this is in Mark 9:21-24

Chapter Nine

Her Mountain Conquered

She made one powerful thrust forward, and in her hand was the garment of Jesus, the master healer.

She felt a sudden change.

Her hemorrhaging was immediately dried up.

I do remember something similar to that taking place. This was in the life of Israel, while on their journey away from Egypt's rigorous bondage.

There was the moment when the great Red Sea was before them, and Pharoah's aggressively pursuing army was after them. Having no other escape route, Moses was told to stretch out his hand (which had a rod) across the sea, and as he did, the Red Sea dried up, providing safety to the Hebrews, but death to the pursuing army, for it swallowed them all up.

Jesus, knowing that something had taken place, sharply turned around in the crowd, asking the question; "Who touched my clothes?" Mark 5:30(b)

"Who did that?" He asked.

What is He talking about? The disciples responded.

I am lost here, someone said.

Will someone please tell me what is going on here? Another one asked.

Nobody did anything as you supposedly think.

Jesus! Are you okay?
Is everything alright with you? Someone further asked.
So many people are here, with the crowd becoming even greater, and you ask such a question. As a matter of fact, you are the reason why this crowd is behaving the way it is. Everyone wants to get close to you, so there is going to be pushing and shoving.

There are so many things one may not, and will not understand, that it should not be surprising with the responses made by others in the midst of a given circumstance or situation.

The apostle Paul who was the most popular and feared persecutor of the Christians in the New Testament times, wrote after his conversion, alluding to Jesus' saying; in 1Corinthians 2:14; "The natural (simple, carnal, unspiritual) mind receives not the things of the Spirit of God, for they are foolishness unto him, neither can he know them, because they are spiritually discerned."

So now we know why they did not understand the reason for Jesus' question. Jesus was saying by the question He asked; someone had just done something which had never been done before.

The touch which I felt is very much different from all of you who have been bouncing and leaning against me. I just, a moment ago, felt virtue leave my body. Someone took something which I did not give, and neither could I have stopped, He said.

Janet Does, from the inception of her quest for healing, wanted to get Jesus' attention. The mountain she had to face, and overcome before doing so, was the crowd of people

She wanted Him to know of her many years of suffering, so her intention was to have a face, to face talk with Him like everyone else who sought His personal attention.

She wanted Him to know that, all the physicians she visited were unable to help her.

All those expectations changed as she pressed her way through the growing crowd.

I cannot fail now, she might have said.

She had no intention of reaching this far in her quest, and not be healed. Absolutely not!

Retreat was not something she had given consideration to, and did not; not at that time.

It does not matter how one think, or what others say of me at this time, she might have said.

There was a famous songwriter, Donnie McClurkin who penned the words of a song which words are;

"I've come this far by faith, leaning in the LORD. Trusting in His holy word, He never failed me yet. Ooh, ooh, ooh, ooh, ooh; I've come this far by faith."

Those words, possibly fueled her spirit as it does to mine, and can do to yours. Suddenly, she felt the change sweeping all over, and flooding her entire body. She has now become the happiest woman in Palestine. Her disposition changed quicker than the speed of light.

It was Jesus who said in the book of Matthew 11:28, giving everyone the invitation to freely come unto Him.

"Come unto me all of you who labor, and are heavy laden (burdened), and I will give rest unto you." Verse 29, says; "Take my yoke unto yourself, and learn of me, for I am meek (gentle, humble, patient) and lowly in heart, and you will find rest unto your souls."

The great prophet Isaiah wrote in his appeal to the Jews said; "Ho, every one that thirsteth, come ye to the waters, and he that hath no money; Come ye, buy, and eat; yea, come, buy wine and milk without money and without price.

Why do you spend for that which is not bread, and you labor for that which satisfieth not? Hearken diligently unto me, and eat ye that which is good, and let your soul delight itself in fatness." Isaiah 55:1-2

No more ashamed of her former condition, she had something to give God praise for. No more feeling resented, or intimidated by anyone anymore, she stood bravely with the crowd.

She did not continue shying away from those in whose presence she was. The people in her neighborhood became very curious, regarding the sudden change in her behavior. She had no more reason to be ashamed. They did not know the reason for the sudden change in her appearance, and demeanor.

Making it more troubling to them, they did not notice any male figure entering, or leaving her house.

They had no reason to say she was engaged, or married, because they did not see an engagement ring, or a wedding band.

She was not driving a BMW (chariot), but continued walking through the dusty roads of Palestine, as she has been doing all of her life, to and from her destination.

Feeling her youthful self again, she developed a new talent; one of singing.

Someone finally asked her the ultimate question; why are you so happy; all of a sudden?

She responded with a testimony in song; "Oh it is Jesus, yes it is Jesus. It is Jesus, in my soul. For I have touched the hem of His garment, and His blood has made me whole."

Janet Does, now healed of her disease, influenced much curiosity from everyone who knew her.

Like the journalist and media personnel, they pelted her with their questions.

Her response was with the burst of a medley; I am delivered, praise the Lord. I am delivered, glory to His name. "Free, free, free; I have been set free; Since I've met the man, that man from Galilee. He set me free, one day, He set me free. He broke the bands of prison for me. I'm going by my Jesus you see, glory to God, He set me free; I'll never be the same again, oh no; I'll never be the same again, oh no. Since my life has changed, I am not the same, oh I'll never be the same again."

As for fashion, she soon developed a likeness for the styles, something she was famous for before her twelve years in seclusion.

Her curious observers did not yet know of her encounter with Jesus, other than what she told them.

The crowd, even Jesus' disciples failed to discern the ministry of Christ's mission.

Do you not know how I know, and why I asked; "who touched my clothes?"
Are you so short of memory? Do you not remember when I chose you twelve?

Jesus was making reference to the identical experience He had, soon after choosing His disciples; "when all those who were diseased; from Judah and Jerusalem, also from the sea coast of Tyre and Sidon, came to hear, and to be healed by Him." Luke 6:13-19.

As far as Janet Does was concerned, she did not touch Jesus, but his clothes. At that time, she had sufficient faith to believe that, just touching something of Jesus will be enough to effect healing to her body.

Too many folks; church folks believe in the preacher, and not in Him whom the preacher represents

Many believe that, if the preacher do not lay his/her hand on their forehead, or shoulder, even that affected part of the body, and pray, healing will not be. They turn away dejected. If special attention is not given to them, healing will not come through.

There are those who believe they must drop to the floor in order to be healed. If that has to be done, then there are questions to be asked. "Are such individuals possessed by a dumb and deaf spirit like that man as mentioned in scripture? Mark 9:17-27. Does one believe in Jesus Christ for their healing/deliverance or believe in falling to the floor?

If it is the latter, then fall to the floor. However, doing that will not give you the healing you are seeking for, But faith in that which Jesus said, and that which he did on the cross.

I am not speaking about an action taken by the Holy Spirit to have someone fall to the floor, where he/she can be more easily worked on.

Some people are so stubborn, and emotional, that even God has to knock them down to keep them still.

I am speaking of a concept, or the mind-set of some who seek God's touch.

The scripture says of the woman with the issue of blood, that she touched the hem of Jesus' clothes. She was delivered of her sickness because she touched him. He did not touch her, but she did him. Neither did she fell to the earth. Her faith did it.

Woman, thy Faith has made thee whole.

Isaiah declared, speaking of Jesus Christ in chapter 53:3-5; "He is despised and rejected of men, a man of sorrows, and acquainted with grief, and we hid as it were our faces from him. He was despised, and we esteemed him not.

Surely he hath borne our grief, and carried our sorrows, yet we did esteem him stricken, smitten of God, and afflicted.

But he was wounded for our transgressions, he was bruised for our iniquities; the chastisement of our peace was upon him, and with his stripes we are healed."

It is for you to trust in Jesus Christ, so that you can receive healing/deliverance.

The author of Hebrews declared in chapter 11:6; "But without faith it is impossible to please Him, for he that cometh to God must believe that He is, and that He is a rewarder of those who diligently seek Him."

Janet, we said was satisfied with touching his clothes; something belonging to Jesus.

Unlike Naaman, who is spoken of in chapter four, expected to stand face, to face with the man of God. He was expecting direct, and special attention; in that Elisha should call upon his God, and strike his hand over the spot of his leprosy, so that he should be healed.

The Roman centurion said to Jesus; "But speak the word only, and my servant shall be healed." Matthew 8:8(b)

You are not going to believe until you feel the touch of His hands.

Allow me to say to you here; "Be it unto you according to your faith."

Chapter Ten

Reconciled To Life, And Living It

Jesus, after His baptism, was walking by the Sea of Galilee where He saw Simon Peter and his brother, Andrew fishing. Jesus said to them; "Follow me and I will make you fishers of men." Matthew 4:18-19

They being His disciples for over two years, did not understand His ministry.

Those who do not know the area of God's calling upon your life in ministry, will at times believe what you are doing does not make sense. Understandably so; they are not the ones called and assigned. The disciples of Jesus Christ had those difficulties themselves, in not understanding how He did ministry.

They are not the one to whom Jesus is speaking, and giving direction.

Too often one believes, the things they do are not seen by anyone.

Too many times individuals do not have knowledge of what we have said, and the places we have been; that without Christ's approval, and even knowledge, would have been classified as one acting out of mere emotions and not faith.

Janet thought Jesus would not have known that she touched His clothes, but she was wrong.

When she brought herself to finding out why the crowd suddenly stopped, she saw Jesus steering straight into her eyes.

With strong feeling, assuming He was angry with her for touching Him without His consent, she bowed/kneeled down before Him, and saying all that had happened. Giving to Him a reason, hoping to justify her action.

She, at that moment in Jesus' ministry became the center of attention. She became Jesus' focus.

Oh; how peaceful; how satisfying; how fulfilling; yes, how honoring it is to know that you are the focus of Jesus. In that, there is a blessing.

Out of fear, Janet Does answered questions that were not asked.
She even told Him some of the things she, and many women will normally feel embarrassed to talk about.
"She told Him all the truth." The whole truth, and nothing but the truth.

Jesus then said to her; "Daughter, thy faith (not mine. This is important to know) has made you whole (well)." In other words, Jesus was saying; I did not do it, but you did.

"Go in peace (not being afraid), and be whole (free) of thy plague (disease)." Mark 5:34

She, I believe was surprised to hear Jesus called her Daughter. She now had a new name, a beautiful name.
The sound of that word in her ears suddenly lifted the burden of fear which was heavily upon her.
All this time, she has been very apologetic to Jesus for touching His clothes, and distracting Him.
All that had changed. She now had a sense of worth, and belonging.

Jesus called her Daughter, while the others, even His disciples scorned, and belittled her.

They were not the ones who were in need.
They were not the ones suffering for twelve long years.
They were not the ones, due to the sickness, are now broke, and penniless.
They were not the ones whom, no one wanted to help.
They are not the ones walking in your shoes, or sleeping on your pillow.

Who else feels your pain, but you?

Hebrews 4:14-15 says; "Seeing then that we have a great high priest, that is passed into the heavens, Jesus the Son of God, let us hold fast our profession. For we have not an high priest which cannot be touched with the feeling of our infirmities, but was in all points tempted like as we are, yet without sin."

When Jesus is attending to you, everyone else will have everything negative and distasteful to say of you. Things they know not of. What a shame.

Who are those people? They are the disciples of Jesus Christ.
They are believed to be children of God.
They go to church on Sundays, or what ever day is designated that they should.
They wear their colorful and neatly fitting suits/outfits.
They, maybe groom themselves twice monthly.
They sing melodiously unto God as claimed.
Are they not the ones who see you as too vile to be in the crowd of which they are a part?
Are they not the ones who, in the past, were just like you, and even worse?
Are they not the ones who, feel Jesus' time is too important to be wasted on you? Yes! They are the ones.

This reminds me of the experience of Jesus with His disciples. The account of which you will find in the gospel of Mark 9:33-40.

In that passage, we understand that Jesus and His disciples were in one's house at Capernaum, and apparently, on their journey there, there was a discussion among them. Who shall be the greatest (most recognized) in the Kingdom of God was the subject of discussion.

Upon reaching their destination, Jesus asked them what they were arguing about.

Jesus then took a little child to Him, and taught them a lesson on humility.

At that point in the discussion, John said to Him; "master, (while we were outside there) we saw one casting out devils in thy name, and we forbade (stopped) him." Luke 9:49

Why did they do that?
They did it because he did not follow, or was not following them.

How many people out there believe you are not true in your walk with Christ, just because you do not follow their direction?

How many people despise you being a child of Christ, just because you do not focus on the things they focus on?

Who were they? They were the disciples of Jesus. They were Christians.

Who stopped the preaching ministry? Christians.
Who despised Janet does? Jesus disciples did.
Who discouraged blind Bartimaeus? The very followers of Jesus; they did.

I recall the apostle Paul in his exhortation to Timothy, said to him; "thou therefore, my son, be strong in the grace which is in Christ Jesus." 11Timothy 2:1

"Endure hardness as a good soldier of Jesus Christ." 11Timothy 2"3

You and I need to do the same thing, and no less.

Daughter, thy faith in Christ Jesus has made you well again. Jesus was literally saying to the woman, He had nothing to do with her deliverance, except that He was at the right place, and at the right time.

He did not know (seemingly) that she was pressing her way through the crowd to touch, even His clothes.

He did not know (seemingly) of her desperation, and that she was not prepared to go back to her house without being healed.

I did not do this ma'am. It was all your own doing.
Your faith, not mine, is what pleased God.

"Go in peace." Do not allow yourself to be bothered by what others think or may; and sometimes do say of you. Now that you are whole (well), you have all reason to be happy. Therefore, rejoice and be glad in it.

Others would have preferred seeing you in your former, sick condition. That would have brought a smile to their hypocritical countenance, seeing you in that state which they have always known you to be in.

God gave His Son, so that humanity can become different.

Jesus Christ came unto us to effect change in our lives.

Our relationship with Christ, in God is all about change.

Change of direction; Matthew 7:13-14
Change of destination; Matthew 7:41
Change of ownership; Romans 6:16
Change of lifestyle; Galatians 5:16-17
Change of nature; 11Corinthians 5:17

Janet Does' faith in Jesus Christ changed the course of her life.

Your prayer, and faith in Jesus Christ, can change your life's course too.

You can press through the storm, and mountains in your life as she did, and touch His clothes. She overcame her mountain, you too, can overcome yours.

Your faith (not the lack of it) in Jesus Christ can make you well again.

Say this prayer. Let it not come from your head, but out of your spirit.

Dear Jesus, I come to you today in reverence, and humility. I consider it a blessed privilege to do so. One which you have given me.

Jesus, I am thanking you for providing healing for me. I now ask you to remove every mountain, every hurdle, every obstacle, every hindrance from my path, so that I can know, and trust you more, without wavering.

Father God, please take away every weight, and forgive me of the sin that has brought on me this sickness which is now a plague to me.

I repent of that sin, and all of my sins, in Jesus name. Amen